Original title:
Tropical Adventures

Copyright © 2025 Creative Arts Management OÜ
All rights reserved.

Author: Alec Donovan
ISBN HARDBACK: 978-1-80581-694-2
ISBN PAPERBACK: 978-1-80581-221-0
ISBN EBOOK: 978-1-80581-694-2

Enchantment Among the Treetops

Swinging from vines, what a sight,
A monkey stole my snack last night.
Tangled in leaves, I take a leap,
Landed in mud, oh, it's a creep!

Bright birds chirp with a cheeky tone,
While I search for my lost phone.
Lizards laugh as they dash away,
I'll chase them down, hip-hip hooray!

Coconuts falling, I duck for cover,
A playful breeze, it makes me shudder.
Parrots gossip with all their might,
"You missed that slip, it was a sight!"

The sun begins to set just right,
I trip on roots in fading light.
With giggles shared and stories spun,
Adventures bloom, oh what fun!

Waves of Laughter

Bouncing on a beach ball, oh what a sight,
Sandy shorts flying like birds in flight.
We stumble and giggle, tip over the tide,
Waves crash in laughter; we can't help but glide.

Seagulls are squawking, stealing our fries,
With saucy little looks, oh, what a surprise!
Chasing them down, we tumble and roll,
In this sunny cocoon, we're losing control.

Sunlit Trails on Golden Sands

Sun-kissed trails lead to ice cream stands,
We run, we shout, leave footprints in strands.
Melting cones slipping, oops, there they go,
A sticky situation, oh what a show!

Flip-flops flapping with each goofy step,
We dance on the shoreline, a beachside rep!
With every misstep, laughter fills the air,
Turns out the sand's quite a slippery affair.

The Island's Heartbeat

Under the palm trees, we strike a pose,
Trying new dance moves that nobody knows.
The DJ's a crab, he plays a fine beat,
With shells as our shoes, we shuffle our feet.

Coconuts rolling, like balls down the hill,
Chasing them fast, what a thrilling skill!
We stumble and giggle, a comedic chase,
The island's heartbeat, a warm, funny place.

Feathered Friends and Ocean Breezes

Cockatoos squawking, giving fashion tips,
As we strut past them with our weird little flips.
Parrots critique our flips and our dives,
While we laugh so hard, we nearly capsize!

The wind tangles hair, a glorious mess,
Feathers and laughter create quite the fest.
With every snicker, a wave rolls in,
In this comedy show, everyone's a win.

Embrace of the Island Waves

The locals dance, their feet so quick,
As waves come in, they take a trick.
I tried to join, but tripped on sand,
The ocean laughed, it had it planned.

A coconut fell, it hit my head,
I swore it spoke, then off it sped.
A parrot cackled, oh what a tease,
I told it my secrets, it laughed with ease.

The sun went down, the stars went bright,
I chased a crab, what a silly sight.
It danced away, I found my shoe,
Oh island life, what else is new?

With ice-cream dreams, I ate too fast,
And now I'm stuck, my fun won't last.
A wave rolled in, my giggles burst,
Oh how the ocean quenches thirst!

Echoes of Tiki Tales

In a dim-lit hut, the stories flow,
Of lost treasure, and a tiki show.
I drank a drink with too much rum,
And thought I'd dance, but fell with a thud.

The drums beat loud, I waved my arms,
A hula girl said, 'You've lost your charms!'
The fire burned bright, but my heart sank low,
As I spun around in my grass skirt glow.

A giant lizard joined the cheer,
His dance was wild, I had to steer clear.
I tripped on my words, and spilled my drink,
The lizard laughed, and I had to wink.

But after the chaos, laughter prevailed,
As tales grew tall, my fears had failed.
With tiki torches lighting the night,
I found my joy, and lost my fright!

Mystical Monsoon Nights

The rain came down, a pitter-pat,
I dodged puddles, just like a cat.
The thunder rumbled, a jungle band,
I mustered courage and took a stand.

With flashlights dancing, we chased our dreams,
The mud was slick, we slipped like beams.
A frog croaked loud, a comic relief,
I slipped on the ground, turning disbelief.

My friends all laughed, amidst the gale,
A paper boat won, we set our sail.
We raced down streams, what a silly sight,
Splashing through puddles, oh what delight!

The storm soon passed, the stars came alive,
In a world of giggles, we began to thrive.
With memories made of laughter and light,
Those mystical nights were sheer delight!

The Dance of Fireflies at Dusk

As dusk fell down, the fireflies spark,
I twirled and spun, embraced the dark.
A mosquito buzzed, I swatted too late,
But the lights kept dancing, it was fate.

A childlike twirl, I jumped with glee,
While dodging bugs, I fell by a tree.
The fireflies giggled, their glow sincere,
"Come join the dance!" they said with cheer.

I caught a glow in my cupped hand tight,
It winked and vanished, oh what a sight!
With laughter echoing throughout the glade,
In a game of chase, I was unafraid.

The night wore on, with sparks in my eyes,
As fireflies formed whimsical skies.
With mischief and light, we danced so free,
The magic of dusk, just you and me!

The Breeze's Gentle Caress

A coconut fell with a thud,
It bounced right off my friend's bare foot.
We laughed until we nearly cried,
As seagulls joined in, quite astute.

The sunburns danced on our pale skin,
While crabs pretended to be shy.
They scuttled past our beach ball gang,
With a wave and wink, oh my!

A frisbee soared, but took a dive,
It landed in a kid's ice cream.
The joy of mess, oh what a laugh,
Who knew we'd all become a team?

With sandy toes and goofy grins,
We've spotted dolphins, just a fluke!
Bikini woes and belly laughs,
This beach day's quite the charming nuke!

Beneath the Cinnamon Sky

We set sail on a banana boat,
With squeals and splashes, off we went.
The captain's hat flew through the air,
As everyone cried, 'What's the scent?'

A parrot squawked a pirate tune,
While monkeys had a dance-off too.
We joined their jam, swung from the trees,
Wearing leaves and mud, what a view!

With cinnamon winds, we marveled wide,
Gazing at giraffes on the shore.
They poked their heads, quite curious,
Thinking we were fruit, what a lore!

As sunset melted, colors mixed,
We feasted on tacos in the night.
Our laughter echoed through the waves,
Beneath the sky, so bold and bright!

The Sound of the Fading Tides

The ocean whispered tales old and new,
As stars twinkled and waved goodbye.
We built our castles, grand and tall,
Until a wave said, 'Not so high!'

There once was a fish that told a joke,
That left us gasping for our breath.
We laughed so hard, we knelt to sea,
But the punchline met a fishy death!

The tide rolled in, it fancied change,
Swirling seashells, a whimsical find.
We chased our dreams in the foam and salt,
While time slipped by, quite unrefined.

With happy shrieks, we rode the waves,
Surfboards dancing, wild and free.
Oh what a night, a blend of sound,
As the moon winked at you and me!

Footprints in Fuchsia Sand

With every step in fuchsia fine,
My flip-flops flew, they took a leap.
They landed near a crab parade,
Who danced around without a peep.

A beach ball bounced off Johnny's head,
His face turned red, a rosy hue.
We laughed so hard, we tipped our hats,
As seaweed tried to join the crew.

Sand angels made, but we forgot,
To check for shells and creepy things.
We squealed as crabs took off in fright,
While seagulls plotted all their schemes.

So here we are, in carefree joy,
With sticky hands and silly minds.
The sun sets low, our day must end,
But in our hearts, the laughter rhymes.

Journeying to Serenity

We boarded a plane, oh what a sight,
With snacks piled high, everything's right.
A penguin in shorts took the aisle seat,
Said he'd trade fish for more tropical treats.

The pilot announced, 'Hang on, folks!'
We laughed as our drinks flew, spilling like hoax.
A parrot gave directions, squawking so loud,
We cheered, and waved to the confused cloud.

As we landed, the palm trees danced,
With sunburned tourists, there was no chance.
A lizard donned sunglasses, struck a pose,
While we fought with sunscreen, oh where did it go?

By sunset we laughed, the day's joys a mix,
Who knew traveling could come with such tricks?
With giggles and smiles, our hearts were so free,
Every mishap transformed into glee.

Spice and Bloom

In a market so bright, full of zest,
A monkey stole fruits, giving us jest.
He tossed us a mango, then made a face,
As if to say, 'You can't keep up with my pace!'

The chili was hot, made noses run wild,
A grin from the vendor, just look at his style!
A parrot chimed in, offered me tea,
I sipped and then coughed, almost lost my glee.

With spices and laughter, we danced through the stalls,
Falling over bananas, oh how we'd have ball!
A chef dropped his apron, slipped on some thyme,
We clapped and we giggled—it felt just like rhyme.

As the sun set behind the fruit-laden trees,
We left with our spoils and bellyful pleas.
Every taste was a joke, every flavor a thrill,
In this crazy market, we found our own quill.

Rhythms of the Rainforest

In the heart of the forest, drumbeats unite,
A sloth served as DJ, what a funny sight!
Beetles formed conga lines, wiggling so slow,
While toads croaked the bass, in colorful flow.

The vines did the tango, each twist full of flair,
A rhythm so quirky—it floated the air.
Frogs started to hop, with kicks of grand style,
They pulled off a jig that would make anyone smile.

Then came a bright toucan, chirping the tune,
He swirled through the branches like a feathered balloon.
While we laughed at the chaos, we joined in the fun,
This rainforest bash was second to none.

With raindrops as confetti, we danced with delight,
As darkness settled, everything felt just right.
In this forest so silly, where laughter entwined,
Our memories were bobbing, joyfully designed.

Lush Horizons Await

Woke up in a hammock, tangled in dreams,
Where roosters were wrestling, or so it seems.
A coconut fell, hit someone on the head,
Laughter erupted, 'Looks like we're fed!'

As we trekked through the greens, paths twisted and turned,
A goat in a hat left us quite concerned.
It strutted with pride, as if it could lead,
Guiding us straight to where adventure would breed.

The waterfall roared, but we slipped in style,
Screens played a movie as we floated a mile.
Squeaky ducks were honking, sounding quite grand,
'You're the best trip companions,' we laughed on the sand.

As night draped the skies and stars twinkled down,
We whispered our secrets, shared laughter, no frown.
In this playful land where all dreams relay,
We promised to return—yes, someday, hooray!

Fallen Leaves of the Tropics

In shades of green, they wiggle and flop,
The dancing leaves, they never do stop.
A monkey snickers, hanging on high,
As leaves fall down like a ticklish pie.

A toucan swoops with a wink and a squawk,
Playing hide and seek behind the tall rock.
With every gust, the chaos ensues,
As leaves scatter like colorful shoes.

Giggling crabs scuttle, oh what a sight,
Chasing the breeze from morning till night.
Each fallen piece tells a tale of cheer,
In this wacky world, we hold so dear.

So join the fun, let your worries go,
In sunny delight, let laughter flow.
We'll dance on the leaves that fall from the trees,
In our merry land, where we do as we please.

Tide Pools and Secrets Untold

In puddles of wonder, creatures abound,
With goofy faces they play all around.
A crab with a hat, so dapper and neat,
Calls out to a fish, who dances on feet.

Oh, sea stars giggle, each one wears a grin,
Tickling the water, inviting you in.
A jellyfish juggles with moves so sublime,
While snails take their time, slow and in rhyme.

Seashells whisper secrets, oh what a jest,
"Join in our fun, we're truly the best!"
A splash from a wave and a shout from a bird,
Life's a big game, every voice must be heard.

So plunge in the tide pools, don't miss out the chance,
Let the sea creatures lead you in their dance.
With laughter and joy swirling all around,
In these magical waters, delight can be found.

Whispering Seashells on the Shore

Seashells chatter in a curious way,
Sharing their tales from night until day.
One claims to have seen a mermaid parade,
While another sings songs that are somewhat decayed.

A conch shell sports a most dashing hat,
"Who wants to join me?" it proudly sat.
With each breeze that blows, the laughter is high,
As seagulls all dance and the crabs just sigh.

The tide rolls in with a tickly touch,
Making the shells giggle, oh so much!
A snail joins the party, wearing a cape,
"I'm the fastest around, just look at my shape!"

Join the merriment, hear the shells sing,
Under the sun, let your heart take wing.
With grains of sand tickling your toes,
These whispers of joy are all that one knows.

Infusions of Spice and Sunshine

In kitchens bright, where colors collide,
Spices jump in with a zesty tide.
A curry pot bubbles with giggles galore,
While mangoes take turns doing the floor.

Papayas wink from the counter so bold,
Whispering secrets of flavors untold.
Chilies play tag with a citrusy fizz,
Stirring up fun in a warm, sunny whiz.

Maracas shake from jars on the shelf,
The rhythm of dinner, amusing itself.
"Come eat with us, we'll make you delight,
With spice and with laughter, we're quite the sight!"

So savor the dishes, let giggles arise,
In a banquet of joy that's sure to surprise.
With every bite, take a trip down the lane,
Where spice meets sunshine, and fun is the gain.

Whispers of the Emerald Grove

In the jungle, monkeys swing,
Telling tales of the bling.
Parrots squawk a silly song,
As we dance the days along.

Lizards sunbathe with a grin,
Feeling fab in their green skin.
Frogs hop by in a parade,
All for fun, no charade!

Coconuts fall with a thud,
Counting counts of the nutty flood.
We laugh until our bellies ache,
Wishing for a giant cake!

In this grove, joy finds its way,
Every moment, a game we play.
The emerald leaves, a playful scene,
Nature's laughter, forever keen.

A Dance Beneath the Palms

Under palms, we start to sway,
Dancing monkeys make our day.
Coconuts bounce like little balls,
While the laughter just enthralls.

Crabs in hats, they strut so bold,
Their tiny moves a sight to behold.
While we join in the merry spree,
Swaying like grass, wild and free.

A parrot dressed in vibrant threads,
Speaks of dreams in tiny heads.
We spin and twirl, a right good show,
As the wind plays a cheeky blow.

Underneath the starlit dome,
We find giggles call us home.
In every dance, the world seems bright,
While the palms sway in delight.

Secrets of the Sapphire Shore

Waves crash gently on the sand,
With a surfboard in our hand.
Seagulls dive for invisible snacks,
As we laugh and dodge their tracks.

Shells like treasures in the sun,
Each one sparkles, oh what fun!
We build castles, tall and wide,
Ready to ride the tide with pride.

A crab winks from his sandy lair,
Waving claws without a care.
Shrimp in shades, they join the crew,
To dance beneath the ocean blue.

Secrets shared in salty air,
With every giggle, we declare.
This shore holds tales of laughter's might,
Each moment shines, pure delight.

The Siren's Call at Dusk

As the sun sinks, the sea unfolds,
Mermaids sing of treasures untold.
With a wink, they splash and play,
Inviting us to join their fray.

Fins and laughter fill the tide,
Sea creatures put their worries aside.
Starfish join in on the fun,
Twinkling brightly, everyone.

Crashing waves with a comic twist,
Seagulls dive for fish they missed.
In the dusk, we dance along,
To the siren's playful song.

Under stars, the night is bright,
With every splash, we take flight.
The ocean laughs, and so do we,
In this world of jubilee.

A Starlit Voyage Over the Ocean

Under the moon's glowing beams,
We set sail on wobbly dreams.
Fish sing shanties, oh what a sight,
As seagulls plot to steal our bite.

The compass spins, oh what a fuss,
Is that a shark or just a bus?
Mermaids giggle, they throw us a line,
Catching tuna is quite a sign!

The captain's hat flies off in the breeze,
And our crew? Just a bunch of bees.
We toast with coconuts under stars,
While hiccuping tales of 'what are we, Mars?'

The waves dance like they're out of control,
We end up in jellyfish roles,
But laughter fills the salted air,
On this voyage, we haven't a care.

Enchanted Isles of Serendipity

In a land where pineapples wear hats,
We stumble upon some talking cats.
They teach us to dance in the sand,
Whiskers flailing, oh what a band!

Palm trees sway like they lost a bet,
While coconuts act like a safety net.
We try to surf on a sea turtle's back,
But end up with seaweed on our snack.

A parrot yells, 'You are all too loud!'
As we dance on the shore, feeling proud.
Frogs in sunglasses join our parade,
Oh, this island's quite a charade!

When the sun sets, we roast some s'mores,
Dancing with crabs, making new scores.
Life here is a spark of pure delight,
In this isle, we forget all our fright.

The Dance of the Sea and Sky

Up in the clouds, a walrus jives,
While dolphins jump and do high-fives.
The sea winks back at the cheeky sun,
And jellyfish twirl, oh what fun!

We gather shells that tickle our toes,
While octopuses perform circus shows.
The horizon pops with laughter and cheer,
As crabs take selfies, how very dear!

The wind plays tunes like a merry band,
As sandcastles rise, so unplanned.
Seagulls fly by, wearing bright ties,
Making sure none of our snacks flies!

The waves keep tickling, what a tease,
As we roll and tumble with the breeze.
In this wild dance of blue and light,
Every moment sparkles, oh what a sight!

Mirage of the Island Dawn

Waking to sunshine, oops, not the norm,
Hammocks broke, what a silly form!
The rooster crows dressed like a king,
While the fish join in for morning bling.

Bananas wear smiles on every tree,
While pineapples giggle, 'Look at me!'
We chase a lizard wearing bright pants,
And end up tangled in a piña colada dance.

The tides are sneaky, pulling us near,
We tumble and slip with nothing to fear.
A crab gives a wink, it knows the game,
As we splash 'round calling each other's name.

Oh, the light of dawn is nothing but fun,
With laughter echoing 'til day is done.
In this mirage where joy is the key,
Life's a carnival, come dance with me!

The Call of the Wild Hibiscus

In the land where flowers talk,
Bumbles bees do silly walks.
A hibiscus winks, bright and bold,
Whispers secrets of the gold.

Sipping nectar, all the fuss,
Listen close, you'll hear a cuss.
A naughty parrot drops a beat,
On his shoulder, a bug to eat.

Every flower's got a quirk,
Dancing leaves just want to jerk.
In this garden full of smiles,
Even cactus wears some wiles.

So join the fun, embrace the bloom,
Don't forget your sunhat's room.
With every laugh and every cheer,
Wild hibiscus draws you near.

Journey Through the Jungle Canopy

Swinging vines and cheeky bats,
Monkeys wearing tiny hats!
Sneaky snakes in a playful scheme,
Hiding where the shadows gleam.

The toucan sports a funny beak,
With a joke that's quite unique.
Riding on a sloth's slow back,
Laughing as they start to snack.

Frogs croak tunes of silly glee,
Who knew swamp life could be free?
A parade of critters winks,
In this jungle, no one thinks!

So take a moment, slip away,
Let the jungle have its say.
With laughter bouncing through the trees,
Adventure calls upon the breeze.

Serene Shores and Starry Nights

Under stars, the crabs got moves,
A dance-off that simply grooves.
Palms sway gently, play the part,
Whispering secrets from the heart.

Seagulls quirk, their feathers wild,
Belly flops? Oh, they've compiled!
As fish pop up for a surprise,
In this laugh-filled sea of skies.

The moon joins in with gleeful jokes,
While dolphins dance, they're no hoax.
Enjoying splashes, giggles rise,
As nighttime sparkles in the skies.

So lay back down, let shadows play,
Join this beachy cabaret.
With waves like laughter rolling bright,
Together, we'll soar through the night.

Lush Lullabies of the Lagoon

In the lagoon where legends sway,
Frogs serenade end the day.
A turtle dons a silly grin,
As playful fish all toss and spin.

With every splash, a giggle bursts,
Crickets chirp their charming blurs.
The dragonflies buzz jokes so cheeky,
Swirling like they're feeling freaky.

A hammock strung between two trees,
Rocking gently with the breeze.
Here lullabies bloom bright and clear,
Where joy and laughter cling so near.

So close your eyes and drift along,
To the charm of nature's song.
In the lagoon, let your heart play,
Silly dreams will save the day.

Starlit Nights over Coral Reefs

Under the stars, fish dance and swing,
A parrotfish sings, doing its thing.
Seashells giggle as tides roll by,
While crabs engage in a crabby high five.

Jellyfish glow as if they're on stage,
A clownfish jests—such a funny fish page.
Octopus hiding with a wink and a wave,
Silly sea creatures, the ocean's own rave.

Sea cucumbers play hide-and-seek,
While starfish flaunt their five-arm mystique.
Sandcastles tumble at the tickle of tides,
In this underwater world, joy never hides.

With laughter echoing through coral halls,
Even a sea urchin has funny sprawl balls.
When the sun rises, and night takes its leave,
We'll laugh at the tales the waves weave and weave.

Journey through the Canopy

Swinging through branches, a monkey doth grin,
He drops his banana, oh where to begin?
Parrots are gossiping, bright colors abound,
While sloths take their time, quite slow on the ground.

A toucan might quack, say 'How do you do?'
While frogs play the drums in a rainy green zoo.
The jaguar naps while the lemurs take bets,
The canopy's gossip rivaling the best.

Vines entangle our feet as we dash,
And a curious raccoon hides chocolate stash.
With giggles and squeaks, we're lost in the fun,
In this leafy playground, behold everyone run!

At night, the owls hoot, sharing their stories,
Of daring old squirrels and nighttime glories.
Through the canopy's charm, we dance and we play,
In this jungle gym life, we'd wish it to stay.

Breeze-Kissed Dreams

Kites in the sky, how they dance in the breeze,
While kids with ice cream enjoy summer's tease.
A parrot swoops down, steals a bright hat,
Now we're all laughing, oh silly old brat!

With the sun setting low, it's a magical sight,
As fireflies flicker, lighting up the night.
We run through the fields till our feet start to ache,
Each moment's a giggle, and oh what a cake!

The waves roll in with a splash and a cheer,
Sandcastles crumble, but we've nothing to fear.
A crab scuttles by, with a wink and a wave,
In this breezy dream, we're all feeling brave.

As stars twinkle bright, and the night takes its claim,
We'll remember these giggles, and nothing's the same.
In the breeze-sweet embrace, our hearts take flight,
We'll dance among starlight, till morning's first light.

Echoes in the Jungle Canopy

A trumpet blast signals the start of the race,
With elephants splashing water all over the place.
Monkeys throw coconuts, giggles all around,
As the jungle erupts with such silly sound.

Parrots squawk tales of the week's biggest heist,
A toucan joins in, each tale is a feast.
Lizards compete in a dance on the run,
In the jungle disco, oh boy, it is fun!

The sound of the drums makes the rhythm feel right,
While snakes do a shimmy, all wrapped up tight.
A jaguar's in stitches, with laughter galore,
In this wild canopy, who could ask for more?

As the day fades away and whispers come clear,
All echoes of laughter will forever stay near.
In the heart of the jungle, where joy knows no bounds,
The power of fun in each heartbeat resounds.

Wandering Through Wildflower Fields

In fields where wildflowers play,
Bees crash like planes, come what may.
A rabbit hops, with style and grace,
I trip and fall, oh what a face!

Butterflies dance like they know the beat,
I try to follow, but trip on my feet.
They giggle and swirl, poor me in a huff,
I swear next time, I'll act a bit tough.

Daisies smile as I tumble around,
The sun gives me kisses, I fall to the ground.
Silly ants march, parade in a line,
While I throw a fit, sipping soda, feeling fine.

As dusk approaches, my adventure's near done,
Birds serenade me, oh, what quirky fun!
I'll smile at this day, albeit a bit clumsy,
In fields of wildflowers, it's hard to feel grumpy!

Serenade of the Swaying Vines

Among the vines, I do a jig,
One jumps out, calls me a twig.
With branches that sway, they join my dance,
I stumble and fall, oh what a chance!

A parrot laughs, squawking with glee,
"What's wrong with you? Just look at me!"
I try to mimic, but squeak like a mouse,
The vines just chuckle, "You're quite a louse."

Swinging from leaves, I lose my grip,
Caught on low branches, oh dear, I slip!
The flora rejoices, a carnival show,
As I wave my arms like a wobbly pro.

At last, I sigh, as night draws its fun,
With stars above, the laughter's not done.
Among swaying vines, I'll rest what I can,
Tomorrow, I'll twirl like a funky man!

Majestic Mountain Paths

Up the mountain, my sneakers squeak,
Each step feels like a clumsy freak.
The rocks are my friends, oh what a crew,
But they trip me up, 'fore the view comes through.

A squirrel watches, I'm sure he will chat,
"Are you lost there, buddy? Just look at that!"
I wave back awkwardly, out of breath,
Climbing for glory, or maybe my death?

The wind gives me hugs, which I don't appreciate,
It shoves me sideways, "Oh, isn't this great?"
I ponder the summit, so close and yet far,
Yet, I chuckle thinking, is there a snack bar?

At the peak, there's a view, such a sight to behold,
I promise next time, I'll think before bold.
With mountains and memories, I'll sit for a while,
Then trip on my way down, and laugh with style!

Searching for Lost Treasures

With a map and a shovel, I start my quest,
Hoping to find gold, oh, wouldn't that be best?
The X marks the spot, I dig with delight,
Only to find mud—what a messy sight!

As I dig deeper, included is mold,
A cheeky raccoon says, "That's old gold!"
I chase him away, but he's got some flair,
With a treasure twice lost, at least he did care.

A crab wears a crown, claims it's a gem,
I laugh at my luck, I'm stuck in this whim.
He snaps at my shovel, a guardian mad,
"Alright, alright, I'll step back, don't be sad!"

To wrap up my search, I find a lost sock,
Declaring it treasure to my astonished flock.
With laughter and stories, I bid adieu,
Maybe next time, I'll know just what to do!

Echoes of the Island Heart

A parrot stole my sandwich, quick!
He squawked and danced, what a funny trick!
I chased him round a palm tree tall,
While locals laughed, I took a fall.

In flip-flops slapping, I found my groove,
The ocean's rhythm made me move.
With a coconut in hand, I strutted by,
Hoping no one saw me slip and fly!

A crab in shades had quite a scene,
He waved his claws like a movie queen.
I took a selfie, feeling grand,
But he pinched me, oh, that little band!

Now on this island, so free and wild,
I'm the laugh of the shore, the beach's child.
With goofy tales I'll share with glee,
Echoes of my heart still float at sea.

Treasure Beneath the Waves

With snorkel fins, I took the plunge,
In search of gold, I had a hunch.
But all I found was old flip-flops,
And a fish that danced, oh how it hops!

The treasure map led me all around,
To sunken cans, oh what a sound!
Each bubble I blew made me giggle,
While fish swam by, doing a wiggle.

A pirate crab, he clapped his claws,
I laughed so hard I dropped my jaws.
He stole my lunch and ran away,
I guess it's hard to eat and play!

So here's to treasures, salt, and tide,
The real gold's the fun, I cannot hide.
With fins and flippers, joy we crave,
In silly depths, we find our wave.

Shadows of the Banyan Tree

Underneath the banyan shade,
I watched a monkey dance, unafraid.
He juggled fruit, a sight to see,
While I just sat with iced sweet tea.

The breeze brought laughter, quite a sound,
As kids played tag and tumbled round.
I tried to join but tripped on roots,
Falling face-first, lost in my boots!

A lizard ran, quite a sprightly cheer,
I swear he winked when I drew near.
With mischief eyes, he made his run,
While I just blinked—oh, what a fun!

In these shadows, life's a joke,
With laughter ringing, hearts bespoke.
Under banyan's arms, we play,
Making memories, come what may.

The Colorful Chorus of Paradise

In a jungle bright, I found my muse,
With colors bold, my heart to choose.
The toucans sang a silly tune,
While I pranced and danced like a cartoon.

A rainbow fish splashed by with glee,
He wiggled and giggled, just like me.
In every note, joy rang clear,
As creatures swayed with merry cheer.

A sloth named Herb took a lazy stroll,
While I raced past, he chuckled, 'Ah, soul!'
With each silly slip, we shared a laugh,
Creating our own colorful photograph!

So here we dance, with nature's band,
In paradise, we take a stand.
With every hue, a melody bright,
Together we bask in laughter's light.

Dance of the Island Breeze

An island breeze tickles my nose,
A parrot squawks, and then it doze.
Flip-flops flapping, toes in the sand,
Dancing with crabs, now isn't life grand?

Coconuts falling, they bump on my head,
I stumble and laugh, cannot get out of bed.
The locals are watching, they think it's a show,
I wave and I wobble, 'come join in the flow!'

Bright flowers bloom, bees buzz with glee,
I try to catch one but it scoots off with tea.
The sun sets and colors erupt like a feast,
Each sip of my drink, a burst to say "cheese!"

Come join my parade, bring laughter, not stress,
We'll dance till we drop, in this colorful mess.
With seashells as trophies, we'll bask in the day,
Tomorrow we'll party; hey, let's find a toupee!

Secrets of the Coral Cove

In the cove where the water is clear,
Fish wear bow ties, it's quite the career!
I try to dive deep, but I start to float,
A turtle swims past like it's in a boat.

Secrets lurking beneath the bright waves,
Octopuses dancing, they've learned all the raves.
A seaweed sandwich? Oh, what a delight,
It wiggled away; I hope it's alright!

The shells all are whispering tales of the deep,
Of mermaids and pirates, secrets they keep.
I wiggle my toes and do a little jig,
A crab joins in, and he's really quite big!

We laugh as we splash, the sea salty and sweet,
There's treasure and giggles in every heartbeat.
In the cove, we'll hold court, discuss our grand plans,
Between shells and the laughter, all the joy expands.

Rhythm of the Rainforest

In the rainforest where the trees stand tall,
Monkeys throw coconuts; what a great fall!
Slippery vines swing, I giggle and sway,
Can't decide if I'm dancing or just in the way.

Frogs leap in colors, a musical band,
Raining down laughter, it's perfectly grand.
A toucan appears and gives me a wink,
I trip on a vine, "just testing my brink!"

The river is bubbling, it sings like a tune,
Bugs with big hats join in a monsoon.
With every step taken, the jungle will roar,
"Let's host a fiesta, then dance on the floor!"

Even the trees sway, they crack up with glee,
At my clumsy attempts, they all laugh with me.
The rhythm of nature is wild and bright,
In this lush jungle, every day is a delight!

Sunset Over Azure Waters

The sun sinks low, painting skies like a dream,
We gather with laughter, it's quite a loud team.
With candy-floss clouds, so fluffy and pink,
I spill my soda and start to rethink.

The waves dance close, they tease at my feet,
As sand flies in laughter, oh, what a treat!
Seagulls are squawking, they've stolen my fries,
I chase them in circles; oh, what a surprise!

Friends play the ukulele, tunes float in the air,
The sunset is slipping; who's bringing the care?
My flip-flops are missing; they've run off to play,
The ocean's my dance floor as I slip and sway.

With cocktails in hand, we clink with a cheer,
Each sunset a canvas, more vibrant each year.
As stars start to twinkle, we settle down low,
In laughter and waves, the memories will flow.

The Serenade of the Surf

The waves are dancing, a silly ballet,
Flip-flops are flying, what a festive display!
Seagulls are laughing, they steal all the fries,
They swoop and they swirl, oh, what a surprise!

Sunburned sunbathers, all chalky and red,
Trying to tan but just ended up spread.
The lifeguard is snoozing, dreaming of waves,
While sand castles tumble, no one really saves!

Pineapple hats and coconut shells,
Everyone's playing; oh, the stories they tell!
A crab in a race with a kid on the shore,
They tie for the win, oh, who could ask for more?

As the sun sets down, the colors ignite,
With laughter and joy, it feels just right.
So grab your beach towel, join in on the fun,
For this seaside story has only begun!

Beyond the Horizon's Whisper

A boat full of pirates, with ketchup for gold,
They search for the treasure, which never gets old.
The map's upside down, the compass runs wild,
"We're lost!" cries a parrot, a most feathery child!

The dolphins peek out, they giggle and splash,
They tease the crew members with a swift little dash.
While mermaids send bubbles, tickling the crew,
They giggle and tumble, it's all quite askew!

The ocean is chuckling, the waves tell their tales,
Of sailors with mustaches that looked like two snails.
They wrestled a seaweed, it tangled their feet,
And danced like old grandpas, quite light on the beat!

As sunset arrives, and the stars start to peep,
The pirates are yawning; they can't even sleep.
With laughter and whispers, dreams of the sea,
They sail homeward bound with a sigh of glee!

The Colorful Carnival of the Coast

Look at those colors, bright kites in the air,
Kids chasing giggles, no worries, no care.
Cotton candy clouds, and balloons full of cheer,
While sea turtles dance, give a wink and a jeer!

The clowns juggle coconuts, what a sight to behold,
As laughter erupts, and it's more than just bold.
The sandman is sleeping, his shovel misplaced,
He wakes up to giggles, all covered in paste!

A limbo contest, how low can you go?
With flip-flops and laughter, a hilarious show!
The hula hoops wobble, they spin and they sway,
As the conch shells cha-cha and dance by the bay!

As the night settles in, lanterns light the scene,
The glow of the fun makes the ocean gleam.
With music and laughter, the fair never ends,
In this vibrant paradise, wonder ascends!

Bewitched by the Fruits of the Forest

In a jungle so vibrant, the fruits talk and quip,
"I'm the best snack!" says the mango, with a flip.
A berry just giggles, "Hey, I'm sweeter than you!"
While bananas are peeling, in a comedic crew!

Coconuts chuckle, they roll down the lane,
With a splash in the river, they giggle again.
The apples are dancing, with wormy delight,
As the pineapples sway, their tops shining bright!

A durian sneezes, it clears out the trees,
The fruits hold their noses, "Oh, please spare us, please!"
The guavas are plotting a fruity parade,
While everybody laughs, no fruit is afraid!

As twilight approaches, the coconuts sing,
In this forest of humor, joy is the king.
With laughter and sweetness, they settle for night,
In the land of the fruits, everything's just right!

Mirage of the Lost Lagoon

A parrot squawks just for fun,
Dancing shadows in the sun.
Flip-flops stuck in gooey sand,
While jellyfish play air guitar in hand.

An iguana wearing shades, so cool,
Sunbathing like it's just a rule.
A coconut falls right on my head,
I swear that fruit just wants me dead!

Seagulls laughing as they fly,
Stealing chips, oh my, oh my!
The fish are gossiping below,
About the sunburns on my toe.

With a splash, a dolphin dives,
Giggling, the ocean thrives.
In this lagoon, all's a jest,
Adventures here won't let you rest!

Sunset Serenade in Paradise

The sun dips low, a blazing sight,
A chicken dances, what a delight!
Palm trees wave their leafy arms,
While crabs play poker, oh such charms!

A ukulele strums by the shore,
A turtle joins—who could ask for more?
The waves are giggling, rolling close,
As I attempt to mimic a seagull's boast.

Lizards gossip in the breeze,
Whispering secrets with such ease.
Don't trust a fish with tales to weave,
They lie about the nets they leave!

As evening falls, the stars appear,
The ocean hums, a lullaby cheer.
In this place where laughter reigns,
Every sunset surely entertains!

Beneath the Coconut Sky

Beneath a sky of coconut dreams,
Where nothing's ever as it seems.
A crab named Larry reads the news,
While seagulls plot their sneaky snooze.

I chased a monkey for a snack,
He stole my sandwich, that's a fact!
With bananas flying through the air,
This jungle is beyond compare.

The breeze contains a playful tease,
As I dodge falling coconuts with ease.
A lizard wearing tiny shoes,
Winks at me before he snoozes.

Under the palm with drinks so sweet,
I join the dance of my own two feet.
In this mirthful, sun-soaked place,
Life's a funny, wild embrace!

Treasure Maps and Untold Tales

I found a map, oh what a find,
X marks the spot, but I'm blind!
The treasure chest, it's just a prank,
Filled with socks and a rubber plank.

To sail away, I grabbed a raft,
But all I found was a clown's craft.
He juggled coconuts with flair,
As mermaids laughed from the salty air.

Parrots chat about old gold,
The tales they tell are far from bold.
A treasure hunt? Just a wild guess,
It leads to more comic distress.

The island's charm, a tangled yarn,
In this adventure, I'll not be gone.
With every laugh and silly story,
I'll claim this quest in all its glory!

Nibbles and Natives

In a village of smiles, where coconuts roll,
The locals munch snacks, while I lose control.
A tortoise steals chips, oh what a sight,
I chase it in sand, what a hilarious fight.

With mangoes in hand, I slip on a peel,
The natives erupt, they laugh like a reel.
I dance with a parrot, it squawks and it swings,
While searching for snacks, guess who's got my rings?

The drums beat a rhythm; I join in the fun,
Tripping on flip-flops, now I'm on the run.
With every giggle, the sun starts to set,
In this silly paradise, I won't forget!

As nightfall arrives, the fireflies flicker,
I twirl like a fool, but that only gets quicker.
The natives all cheer, "You're part of our crew!"
As I tumble and roll, they say, "Hey, you too!"

Chasing Fireflies of the Coast

Under stars so bright, I chase glowing lights,
With cousin named Bob, oh, what silly sights!
He trips on a shell, and down he goes fast,
Making waves in the sand—oh, he'll be a blast!

The fireflies swirl, like tiny little ships,
We're dodging the waves, taking funny slips.
With nets made of dreams, we stumble and leap,
As squawking seagulls steal snacks we can't keep.

I trip on a driftwood, Bob lets out a shout,
"Catch one for me, mate!" as I tumble about.
Then up pops a crab, it joins in our race,
In the glow of the night, we've found our own space.

The ocean waves clap, as we dance on the shore,
In this caper of fun, who could ask for more?
With laughter and chirps, we swim through the evening,
In chasing those fireflies, we're simply believing!

Pirates of the Forgotten Atoll

Ahoy there, mateys, on an islet so small,
Where treasure is tacos, we'll feast them all!
With eye-patch and cutlass, I sail with my crew,
But our only gold? A burrito or two!

The parrots are gossiping, bickering loud,
As I drop my compass, oh isn't it proud!
We forge through the jungle, a quest for a pie,
When a monkey steals food, oh, my! Oh, my!

With more swash than buckle, we find a fine prize,
A treasure map drawn by a crab, oh, what lies!
We dig with our hands, but it's sand all the way,
And each scoop we take, we laugh more than play.

At sunset we gather, our loot is all weird,
With seashells and snacks, our appetite steered.
With smiles like the sun, we toast to the night,
In this pirate life, oh what a delight!

A Symphony of Exotic Calls

In the heart of the jungle, where the critters all play,
Sounds of the wild keep the worries at bay.
A parrot recites all my secrets, it seems,
While I trip on a vine, and fall into dreams!

The frogs get together, a concert of croaks,
While monkeys swing by, sharing their jokes.
I join in their chorus, with some odd rhymes,
As the sun sets below, all is simply sublime.

The toucan yells "Hello!" in a vibrant display,
While I make funny faces to keep the bugs at bay.
With a flutter of wings and some playful chats,
The jungle holds laughter; we're wearing our hats.

As darkness approaches, the owls start to hoot,
Their wisdom so quirky, who knew it was cute?
Amidst all the calls, we harmonize well,
In this symphony wild, there's magic to tell!

Tides of Time at the Coral Reef

With flip-flops on and sunblock spread,
A crab scuttles by, I dash ahead.
I trip on seaweed, and what a sight,
Flopping like a fish, oh what a fright!

The waves laugh too, as I belly flop,
My sunglasses fly, a beach ball bop.
The fish all giggle, quite the charade,
In this watery world, I'm quite the spade.

A seagull steals my sandwich, oh dear!
I chase it around, no food left here.
With sand in my shoes and salt in my hair,
Life in this paradise is beyond compare.

Finally, I sit, with a cold drink in hand,
Recapping the chaos of this wonderland.
With sunburned cheeks and a heart full of glee,
These tides of time are just perfect for me.

Magic Beneath the Dappled Light

Under palm fronds, I start to sway,
A monkey swings by, stealing my ray.
With laughter echoing through the trees,
He takes my hat, oh just let me be!

The coconuts fall, one lands on my toes,
I dance and I yelp, more than anyone knows.
The sun winks down with a playful gleam,
As I trip on a root, am I part of a dream?

A colorful parrot squawks out my name,
I can't keep a straight face, this is all a game.
With glimmering waters that tease my will,
I dive in headfirst, oh this is a thrill!

Amidst the chuckles of creatures around,
I feel quite the jester; laughter knows no bound.
Under dappled light, in this joyous fight,
Life is a circus, oh what pure delight!

In the Arms of the Sea Breeze

The beach chair's a throne, my cape the towel,
The wind gives a tug, the sea it howls.
A kite takes off, I'm left in its wake,
I chase after dreams, whatever it takes.

An ice cream cone, oh what a treat,
But it melts so fast, drips down to my feet.
I laugh as I lick, what a sticky mess,
In the arms of this breeze, who cares to impress?

Sandcastles rising, but watch for the tide,
In a twist of fate, my castle's denied.
The waves crash down, my kingdom's erased,
I'm just a beach bum, but oh, what a taste!

Yet joy swells up, like the foam on the sea,
With every mishap, I just feel more free.
In the breeze I twirl, round and round I spin,
This seaside adventure brings laughter within!

Sifting Through Golden Sands

Armed with a shovel and a pail in hand,
I dig for treasures in this golden land.
But under the surface, what's lurking below?
A flip-flop surprise, oh where did it go?

With every scoop, there's laughter and cheer,
I find a lost toy, my childhood's still near.
A hermit crab joins, he's stuck in a shell,
We share in the warmth, oh, it's just swell!

Friends in the sand, we gather 'round high,
A sand angel flops, just like a fly.
The sun sets low, painting skies of pink,
In the chaos of joy, it's fun to rethink.

So here in this wonder, with sand in my hair,
I invent my own stories, without a care.
Every sift tells a tale, every grain holds its song,
In this beachy paradise, I've found where I belong!

The Melodies of Mangroves

In mangroves where the crabs dance wide,
A parrot's laugh, it's hard to hide.
Fish flip-flop, do their best ballet,
While slippery eels dive and splay.

A monkey swings, takes a wild trip,
Lands in a boat, gives a silly flip.
With coconuts that roll and greet,
They giggle and jive to the wild beat.

Giant turtles wear sun hats so bold,
Spinning tales that never get old.
A symphony of giggles sings loud,
As each critter gathers, feeling proud.

The breeze acts goofy, pulling on hair,
As the sun plays peek-a-boo with flair.
In this wild band, no one follows rules,
Just laughter echoes, making fools.

Footprints at the Water's Edge

Footprints mark the sandy stretch,
With mystery for a crab to sketch.
Seagulls squawk like they own the show,
As surfboards wobble, putting on a show.

A kid trips, falls, and starts to roll,
Drenched in waves, he's lost his soul.
His friends laugh hard, like it's a sport,
While his wet shirt earns a snorting retort.

Sandcastles topple in big waves' cheer,
A pirate's flag waving, brings a sneer.
The sunburned beach bum takes a dive,
For a cooler drink, he claims to thrive.

Dolphins leap, donning shades so bright,
They join the fun, capturing the light.
As night falls, shadows dance in glee,
Echoing laughter: a wild decree.

Whispers of the Emerald Isle

Emerald trees sway with a grin,
A leprechaun's jig, let the fun begin!
Turtles gossip about secret quests,
While dragonflies wear their fanciest vests.

A parrot shares stories with bold neckties,
While playful monkeys drop by for replies.
A game of tag under the bright sunbeam,
Turns into chaos with a sneaky scheme.

Frogs croak numbers for a raucous cheer,
While crickets chirp, they can't help but leer.
The laughter of fish splashes about,
As they tease a crab, giving a shout.

The fireflies gather for a night's parade,
Lighting up each laugh and escapade.
In this isle full of giggles galore,
Adventure awaits, who could ask for more?

Beneath the Palm Canopy

Beneath the palms, the shadows hide,
Where iguanas wear sunglasses with pride.
A sleepy sloth thinks it's time for a nap,
While crickets play cards, on a leafy map.

A toucan's call is ridiculous and loud,
As he mixes up words to entertain the crowd.
Chasing fireflies, a wild chase ensues,
With giggles erupting like colorful hues.

The sand beneath holds secrets untold,
Shells whisper jokes, if you're brave and bold.
Monkeys throw coconuts, softer than darts,
While laughter bounces, from their merry hearts.

Beneath the palms, life's never quite tame,
A festival of antics, it's quite the game.
Join in the fun, where delight is a rule,
And every moment's a whimsical jewel.

Eyes of the Dragonfly

In the sun, they dart and dive,
With eyes like jewels, they come alive.
Buzzing past with such great zest,
These tiny pilots put skills to test.

They tap dance on a lily pad,
Making frogs feel quite a tad.
A dizzy flight, a swirly spree,
And I'm just here avoiding bees.

Oh, watch them flirt with shady leaves,
Making their way as my heart deceives.
A dragonfly stole my sandwich, you see,
In this picnic bungle, it's just me and a tree.

With laughter ringing through the grass,
These winged jokers really have sass.
Who knew that bugs could be such fun?
In this game of chase, I'm done, I'm done!

Coral Crown on an Island King

A crab in shades, he rules the shore,
With a crown of coral, he'll ask for more.
Waving his claws, he greets the crowd,
In his royal realm, he's ever so proud.

He dances on rocks, with a pirouette,
Looking for fish in a game of roulette.
The seaweed waves as his royal sash,
When he trips in the surf, oh what a crash!

Underwater parties, where jellyfish glide,
He spins in circles, with friends by his side.
But look out, dear king, there's a sponge in the way,
And with one swift move, you're now part of the play!

As sunset glimmers, the beach will erupt,
A king with a crown and a sea turtle pup.
With a giggle and squawk, let the fun begin,
In this wacky kingdom, we'll always win!

Secrets in a Seashell's Song

A shell on the shore has a voice so sly,
Whispers of treasures that swim by.
Oh, the gossip it spills, of crabs and fish,
In a sonnet of bubbles, each wave a wish.

Tune in, dear friends, to the songs of the tide,
Meet the octopus singer with pearls as his pride.
"Squirt and swirl!" he calls, "Join the dance!"
And I trip on seaweed—oh, what a chance!

With laughter that echoes across the wet sand,
We listen and giggle at his zany band.
A walrus on drums, a seahorse ballet,
Who knew that the beach could be this cliché?

The seashell hums its melodious tune,
As our toes become one with the waves and the moon.
Secrets revealed on this shimmering shore,
With oceans of laughter, who could ask for more?

Gardens of Bright Abandon

In a garden where flowers can't seem to sit,
Colors collide—a bustling skit!
Daisies gossip with poppies in pink,
While butterflies flutter, oh what do they think?

The petunias twirl in the festival glow,
Chasing the bees in a lively show.
Each bloom a chatterbox, full of delight,
Whispering tales under twilight's sight.

A rogue tumbleweed rolled by unexpectedly,
"Oh no!" cried the lilies, "Not us, please!" They said.
But the laughter rang true, in this wild floral spree,
A carnival dance, come join, come see!

So here in this patch of chaotic cheer,
Life blooms in colors that we hold dear.
With petals of joy, we twinkle like stars,
In a garden of abandon, there are no bizarre bars!

In Search of the Rainbow Fish

In waters deep where fishies play,
A rainbow's shimmer leads the way.
I chased it fast, slipped on a fin,
Fell in the sea, let the fun begin!

Bubbles burst and laughter soars,
I danced with crabs, dodged slippery doors.
The fish just giggled, flicked their tails,
While I searched for treasure and some whale's gales!

Sun-kissed sand and salty air,
A jellyfish twirls with flair.
I reached for gold, but found a shoe,
Guess treasure hunting's tricky too!

At last, the fish, all colors bold,
Said, "Join us, traveler, join the fold!"
With laughter shared, we swam so free,
A happy fish, that's now just me!

Vulcan's Heartbeat on the Shore

The volcano rumbles, quite a show,
A beachside dance with molten glow.
I brought a snack, it smelled so nice,
But it fell in the lava—oh, how 'bout that slice!

With feet in sand and head in steam,
I tried to keep it cool—my dream.
But lava pops like goofy jokes,
My sandwich transformed—now it smokes!

The locals laughed, "What a mess!
Your picnic, dear friend, is anyone's guess!"
The ash fell lightly like confetti bright,
At this fiery feast, I ate with delight.

So here I toast with a marshmallow roast,
To the volcano, who loves to boast!
With laughter ringing, joy on the shore,
In Vulcan's whimsy, who could want more?

Portraits of Vibrant Flora

In gardens where the colors burst,
I looked for flowers—oh, what a thirst!
With petals bright, and bees in flight,
One tickled my nose, it wasn't polite!

I elbowed a fern, got tangled in twine,
It wrapped me up, I felt divine!
With cacti giggling, my hat went askew,
"Who wore it better?" asked the bamboo.

Sunflowers grinned, as tall as can be,
While daisies whispered, "Come play with me!"
A rose waved petals, so soft and sweet,
But thorns said, "Careful! Don't take a seat!"

In this zoo of petals, I spun and twirled,
My floral friends laughed, my hat was twirled.
Among vibrant hues, we danced the day,
In nature's art show, we laughed and swayed!

Discoveries at Sunset's Edge

At sunset's edge, where skies ablaze,
I found a crab doing a happy phase.
It wore a party hat, a sight so grand,
And invited me to join the band!

We waltzed on sand, it's such a spree,
Dancing with crabs is truly key.
They taught me moves, so slick and quick,
But tumbled headlong—oh, what a trick!

As tweety birds chirped their evening tune,
The crabs performed with a silver moon.
I clapped so hard, feet in the surf,
As wave spills giggled, chuckling with mirth.

At sunset's edge, with crabs and cheer,
We shared silly jokes, from ear to ear.
In this playful dusk, we spun with delight,
Adventures found, hidden in the night!

Between Tides and Time

On a beach where coconuts fall,
A crab in shades begins to sprawl.
Seagulls squawk a silly tune,
While sunbathers toast like the afternoon.

With a splash, a dolphin dives,
Wearing sunglasses, feeling alive.
A fisherman's line gets tangled tight,
As he yells, 'I caught a shoe, what a sight!'

Barefoot wanderers chase the waves,
Sand in their toes, like silly knaves.
A parrot squawks from a palm tree high,
'Why don't we ever fly, oh my!'

As the sunset paints the sky bold,
Laughter echoes, stories retold.
In this land where the silly reigns,
The best adventures hide in the grains.

Flavors of the Tropics

Beneath the shade of a mango tree,
A squirrel sips from a coconut spree.
Pineapple hats and guava beams,
A feast that dances in wild dreams.

On the grill, fish do a little jig,
As someone tries to roast a pig.
With chili laughs and limey glee,
The cook spills soup, like a big ol' spree.

Smoothies burst with colors bright,
But a bee steals a sip, what a fright!
Sipping punch from novelty straws,
While sticky fingers get applause.

In the market, flavors swirl and prance,
Tourists stumble, they join the dance.
Taste buds tickle, a joyful sound,
In this fruity land, fun knows no bounds.

Whispers of a Hidden Cove

In a cove where secrets lie,
A turtle grins, slips on a tie.
Waves whisper to rocks on the shore,
'Why do fish always ask for more?'

With the sun bright as a disco ball,
A crab does the cha-cha, what a haul!
Seashells giggle, hiding their charms,
While tourists flaunt their best sunburned arms.

A pirate frequents the secret spot,
Looking for gold, but finds a pot.
Full of candy and cotton candy dreams,
He mumbles aloud, 'What are these schemes?'

As twilight falls, the fireflies dance,
While beachgoers join the moonlit trance.
In this cove where joy's the song,
Whispers of laughing, all night long.

Singing Stones and Shimmering Seas

Stones that hum with a breezy tune,
Under the light of a winking moon.
Mermaids giggle in the foamy spray,
Counting fish as they flit away.

In the surf, a clam clamps tight,
A crab in a tux dreams of a night.
The tide comes in with a splash and a cheer,
As seaweed crowns them, no need to fear.

Seashells scatter like confetti bright,
While dolphins dance in sheer delight.
A seagull swoops, it steals a fry,
And the diners shout, 'Oh my, oh my!'

As stars twinkle in the ocean's embrace,
Laughter bubbles, a warm-hearted race.
In this world where fun's a breeze,
Singing stones share whimsical keys.

www.ingramcontent.com/pod-product-compliance
Lightning Source LLC
Chambersburg PA
CBHW072131070526
44585CB00016B/1631